GREAT PETS

Snakes

Joyce Hart

 **Marshall Cavendish**
Benchmark

New York

Marshall Cavendish Benchmark
99 White Plains Road
Tarrytown, New York 10591
www.marshallcavendish.us

Library of Congress Cataloging-in-Publication Data

Hart, Joyce, date
Snakes / by Joyce Hart.
p. cm. -- (Great pets)
Includes bibliographical references and index.
Summary: "Describes the characteristics and behavior of pet snakes, also
discussing their physical appearance and place in history"--Provided by
publisher.
ISBN 978-0-7614-2996-8
1. Snakes as pets--Juvenile literature. I. Title.
SF459.S5H37 2008
639.3'96--dc22
2008024333

Front cover: A boa constrictor
Title page: Two corn snakes hatching from eggs
Back cover: A corn snake

Photo research by Candlepants, Inc.
Front cover credit: Biosphoto / Girard Cédric / Peter Arnold
The photographs in this book are used by permission and through the courtesy of: Alamy: Inmagine, 9; Paul Wood, 12;
Chris Mattison, 30; Imagees of Africa Photobank, 38. Photo Researchers: Marc Phares, 6; Joseph T. & Suzanne L.
Collins, 23 (top); A. Cosmos Blank, 23 (bottom); Art Wolfe, 27; Joseph T. Collins, 28. Peter Arnold: Philippe Hays, 14;
John R. MacGregor, 24; Biosphoto / Cavignaux Bruno, 33; Biosphoto / J. L. Klein & M. L. Hubert, 35; Biosphoto /
Cavignaux Regis, 42. AP Images: Jim Lord, 17. Animals Animals/Earth Scenes: Zigmund Leszczynski, 1, 41; C.C.
Lockwood, 29. Getty Images: Chris Windsor, 18, back cover; AFP Photo / Patrick Lin, 22. The Image Works: PRISMA /
V&W, 4; C. Walker / Topham, 7. Shutterstock: Anita Patterson Peppers, 10, 25; John Bell, 16; HTuller, 20; Elan Sablich,
21; Sergey I, 26; RLHambley, 34; Ami Beyer, 37. Corbis: Erik Freeland, 40.

Editor: Karen Ang
Publisher: Michelle Bisson
Art Director: Anahid Hamparian
Series Design by: Elynn Cohen

Printed in Malaysia
6 5 4 3 2 1

Contents

1

Snake Facts

Different types of snakes have lived on the planet for more than 100 million years. Some **species**, or types, of snakes lived alongside the dinosaurs! Despite their long history on the planet, snakes have always been viewed with mixed emotions. Some cultures honored snakes while others portrayed them as evil or dangerous.

One culture that honored snakes was the Aztec people. More than five hundred years ago, they lived in the land that now includes Mexico. Aztecs believed that snakes were connected to the gods. Images and carvings of snakes are shown in artifacts (historical pieces) from that time.

In Greek mythology, the messenger god Hermes carried a staff as a symbol of peace. The staff had two snakes coiled around it. An ancient healer, Asclepius, carried around a staff with a single serpent wound around it. In Ancient Greece, many believed that healers learned to make medicine from

Snakes and serpents were important to the Aztec people. They included snakes in their artwork and architecture.

Different versions of the caduceus have been used through the years. One of the features that remained, however, was the snake or snakes wrapped around the staff.

wild plants by watching how snakes healed themselves. Today, the caduceus is used to symbolize physicians (doctors) and other healers. The caduceus is a winged staff with two serpents coiled around it.

Snakes and serpents were not always respected. In many stories, fables, and myths, snakes were cast as the evil villains. They tricked people, hurt them, and caused other problems. Today, in movies, books, and other media, snakes are still often seen as horrifying creatures that should be feared.

Scary snakes and serpents were often used to represent evil in many stories and legends.

A reasonable fear of snakes is not necessarily a bad thing. There are snakes that can kill people—by squeezing them to death or by biting them. And some snake bites can include a deadly **venom** or poison that can injure and kill. So it is smart to use caution whenever you see a snake in the wild.

LARGEST AND SMALLEST

Pet snakes can range in size, but the world's largest and smallest snakes are not types that are kept as pets. Anacondas are the largest snakes in the world. They live in the swamps of South America. Anacondas can grow to be more than 30 feet (9.14 meters) long, 40 inches (1 m) wide, and weigh more than 400 pounds (181.44 kilograms). Anacondas eat pigs, deer, fish, and a type of crocodile called a caiman.

Two of the smallest snakes in the world include the thread snake and the blind snake. These snakes are so small they look like earthworms. Some of these snakes are less than 5 inches (12.7 centimeters) long. These tiny snakes are found in the warm regions of the United States, such as in Texas. They are so small that they eat the tiny eggs of ants and termites.

Not all snakes are green, brown, or black. Many are red, orange, or a mixture of several different colors. Part of the fun of owning a snake is looking at its interesting scales and skin.

However, the truth is that of all the snakes in the world, only a small portion of them are poisonous. Some snakes, like the giant anaconda in South America, are big enough and strong enough to wrap their bodies around their victims and strangle them. But these are not the kinds of snakes that are kept as pets. There are plenty of other snake species that people can keep in their homes. With proper care these snakes can make interesting and unique pets.

2

Snakes as Pets

When most people hear the word *pet,* they probably first think of a cat, a dog, or something small like a hamster. Though all of these animals make great pets, some people want a different kind of pet. This is where snakes come in. As people learn more about snakes and snake care, these animals are becoming more and more popular as pets.

Snakes make great pets because they do not need a large yard to run around in, though they must have a living space that is big enough for their needs. Snakes do not have fur or hair, so people who sneeze and itch when they are around cats and dogs may consider a snake as a pet. They are not necessarily easier to care for since they do require feeding, cleaning, and check-ups with a **veterinarian.** But you do not have to take your snake out for walks several times a day. Though they can hiss and make a little noise, snakes are very quiet pets.

It is important to remember, however, that snakes are not the perfect pets for everyone. When considering any kind of pet, you should do careful research and really think about how that pet will fit into your life.

For many families, these scaly reptiles are the perfect pets.

When considering whether or not to get a pet snake, you should think about how big it will get and if you will be comfortable holding it and taking care of it.

Is a Snake Right for You?

If you cannot have or do not want a dog, cat, bird, or hamster, should you automatically decide on a snake? Not necessarily. While snakes do get used to their humans—and some long-time snake owners believe that their snakes recognize them—they are not affectionate like some other types of pets. They may curl up in your hand or around your arm, but often that is because it is convenient for them or because they need the warmth from your body. If you are looking for a pet that will learn tricks, fetch things for you, or come up to you for a cuddle or playtime, a snake is not the right pet for you.

Snakes are perfect for some people because they do not need a lot of constant attention. You will, however, have to provide a safe home with everything the snake needs to be healthy. Before you get a snake, think about if you can provide those things.

Do you have enough space? Some snakes do not grow very large and do not require very large cages or **terrariums.** Some will be happy in an average-sized aquarium or tank. Other snakes, however, start out small but can grow to be several feet long. Can you provide a large living space for the snake?

Snakes are cold-blooded animals. Cold-blooded creatures cannot generate enough body heat on their own. In the wild, they will stay in the sun to heat up and go into the shade to cool down. If you keep a pet snake in your home, you must be sure that you can provide it with the kind of environment it needs to maintain healthy body temperatures.

All snakes—even pet snakes—need to eat meat to survive. Depending upon the size and species of your snake, this may mean food as small as crickets and worms to larger food like mice, rats, or even small rabbits. This is what snakes need to eat in order to survive. If you plan on having a snake, you must be sure you are comfortable feeding your pet these kinds of foods.

As with all pets, keeping a snake does cost time and money. You will have to keep its cage clean and make sure that the snake stays healthy—that takes time and patience. Supplies for the snake—especially large snakes—may not be cheap. You must be sure you are willing to spend the money for its supplies. Fortunately, careful planning and smart shopping can help keep some costs down.

Where to Get Your Snake

There are a number of different places to get your snake. Pet stores are the most obvious and convenient choice. Some pet stores carry a wide variety of snakes. However, many experienced snake owners suggest that you look into getting your snake directly from a **breeder.** Breeders often advertise their snakes on the Internet, in snake-themed pet magazines, or in newspapers.

Reptile shows are a good place to meet breeders, look at snakes, and possibly buy your pet. At these shows, breeders and other companies that sell snake supplies display their products and animals. Most of the things they

Reliable pet stores and breeders can tell you exactly what kind of snake you are buying and how old it is.

RESCUE GROUPS

Around the country there are many reptile rescue organizations. These groups are made up of volunteers who try to find home for reptiles—such as snakes, lizards, and turtles—that have been abused or abandoned. The goals of these organizations are to get the pets healthy and then find them appropriate homes. You may consider adopting a snake from one of these groups, but it may not be the best choice for a first-time snake owner. However, the members of these organizations will be the ones to decide if adopting one of their snakes is the best choice for you and the snake.

Most of the reptiles that these groups rescue belonged to people who could no longer care for the pet. Usually, the pet became too large and too expensive to keep. This is why you must always take time to really think before bringing any kind of pet home. Pets are live animals that you must be committed to caring for. If you are not prepared to provide the time and money that long-term pet care requires, you should consider other options.

bring are for sale. A reptile show is a good opportunity for you to look around at different types of snakes. You can see how they look and what they may grow to look like. Pet stores often only have a few types of snakes. At a show you may see dozens of different species in different colors and at different ages. Most importantly, you will be able to ask these experienced snake keepers questions you may have about snakes as pets. Some snake owners also say that buying supplies at a reptile show is sometimes better than buying at a pet store. Some companies sell their products at reduced prices at the shows, and you may have more selection to choose from. Reptile shows are often advertised on the Internet and in snake magazines.

Never catch a snake from the wild and then keep it as a pet. Not all snake species make good pets. Some are endangered, which means that their

wild populations are almost gone. It is illegal, or against the law, to own endangered snakes. Most endangered snakes are not suitable as pets anyway. Others, such as the venomous ones, are dangerous—or even deadly— to keep.

Wild snakes, such as this venomous rattlesnake, should never be taken from the wild and kept as pets.

Besides the fact that you could be bringing in an illegal or dangerous pet, you would be taking the animal away from its natural home. The snake is used to living in the wild, and you would not be able to provide it with the same environment that it needs. Responsible snake breeders never sell wild-caught snakes. The snakes they sell are the offspring (children) of snakes that have never lived in the wild and are used to living indoors in man-made environments. Also, some snake breeders only breed and sell snakes that are ideal as pets. These snakes are easy to handle, are not likely to attack, and most do not require a lot of special supplies. These are the kinds of snakes that are good for a first-time snake owner.

What to Look for

When you have decided where to get your snake, you will want to make sure you are bringing home a healthy pet. Whether you are buying from a pet store or a breeder, be aware of the surroundings. Look at where the snakes are

Before buying or adopting a snake, ask to handle it. A breeder or pet store worker will show you how to properly hold your pet snake.

kept. Do they look like they are given enough clean space? Do the snakes look healthy? How are they behaving? Are they striking out at the glass or the sides of their terrariums? You want to be able to handle your pet, so it would be best to get a calm snake that does not mind being held. Do not be afraid to ask the seller if you can handle the snake.

You should also consider the sellers. Can they answer the questions you have about snake keeping? Do they seem to know a lot about the types of snakes they are selling? How long have they been breeding or selling these snakes? Breeders who seem knowledgeable or who have been breeding snakes for a long time will most likely have healthy animals. You do not want to buy from people who do not know a lot about the snakes they are selling. This would most likely mean that the snakes are not well cared for and may be sick.

Getting your snake from the right place is as important as the snake you actually choose. You want to have a healthy pet and you do not want to give your business to people who do not care for their animals.

3

Types of Pet Snakes

If you have decided that you want a snake as a pet, you now have to choose what type of snake to buy. There are many things to consider when choosing a type of snake. You must think about how much space you have. If you do not have space for a very large terrarium, then you should choose a snake that does not get too big. How often will you handle or hold your snake? If you plan on holding it a lot, then you should consider a breed that is easy to handle. The snake's diet should also be considered. Some types of pet snakes are very picky eaters and have very specific diets. These kinds of snakes are usually not a good choice for first-time snake keepers.

Many snake breeders, as well as people who already own snakes, suggest that the best snakes for first-time snake keepers are corn snakes, king snakes, and milk snakes. These are naturally gentle snakes that do not grow to be too large. Other types of snakes are kept as pets, such as pythons, boa constrictors, and garter snakes. But these are usually recommended for people who have some pet snake experience.

A corn snake is one of the most popular types of pet snake.

Corn snakes can be found in the wild in many places across the United States. Your pet corn snake should come from a breeder or pet store, and not from the outdoors.

Corn Snakes

Corn snakes are the most popular snakes for children and first-time snake keepers. These snakes are popular because they are one of the gentlest snakes to own as a pet. When held properly, they do not usually bite and will be happy to slither around on hands and arms. The corn snake's size also makes it a good pet. An adult corn snake grows to be 3 to 5 feet (.91 to 1.52 m) long. Unlike some other snakes, corn snakes do not need really high temperatures and a lot of moisture. Average daytime and nighttime temperatures for a corn snake should be 71 to 85 degrees Fahrenheit (21.67 to 29.44 degrees Celsius).

Corn snake terrariums tend to be much simpler than terrariums for other snakes. However, they do need a terrarium that is big enough for a full-grown corn snake. (Experts suggest a tank that is at least 30 gallons in size.) They can be good escape artists, so as with any snake, you must make sure that your pet corn snake cannot escape from its home. Corn snakes are more active during the early evening and at night. Like other snakes, corn snakes are carnivores and need to eat meat. So you will need to feed your snake small mice.

Corn snakes are very attractive snakes—some have orange and yellow patterns on their backs and sides. Their bellies usually have a black-and-white checkerboard pattern. But not all corn snakes have the same color or pattern, so if you buy your snake from a breeder, there could be a lot of different types to choose from.

Corn snakes can come in a variety of colors. Some breeders will have a large selection from which you can choose.

However, do not choose your snake only on its color. Also consider its temperament—how it reacts to being held and watched—and whether or not it looks healthy.

King Snakes

King snakes are as gentle as corn snakes, which is why they make good pets. These snakes can grow to be as long as 6 feet (1.83 m). Like corn snakes, your pet king snake will not need very high temperatures or a lot of moisture. King snakes can attack other snakes, however, so you should only keep one snake in a terrarium. The temperatures in your king snake's home should be around 77 to 86 degrees F (25 to 30 degrees C) during the day and 74 degrees F (23.33 degrees C) at night.

King snakes come in many different colors. The most common colors are black or brown with white or yellow stripes. King snakes are most active in the morning and early afternoon and tend to be a little more active than corn snakes. They also will need to eat mice for food.

Most king snakes that have been gently handled will enjoy slithering around on your hand or arm.

A DANGEROUS TWIN

Scarlet king snakes make great pets, but the eastern coral snake—which looks a lot like a king snake—should never be kept as a pet. Eastern coral snakes are very venomous and can cause great injury or death with their bites. These two snakes look alike because they have bands or rings of yellow, red, and black. The arrangement of these colors, however, can tell people which kind of snake they are seeing. The popular rhyme "Red next to black is safe for Jack, but red next to yellow will kill any fellow" is used to remember which snake is which. Scarlet king snakes have red rings next to black rings. Eastern coral snakes have red rings next to yellow rings.

In different parts of the United States, you may run into eastern coral and scarlet king snakes in the wild, but do not try to touch one even if you are sure it is a king snake. You should only ever touch a king snake when it is a pet that is definitely a king snake.

If you are not looking very closely, a scarlet king snake (top) and an eastern coral snake (bottom) look very similar.

Milk snakes got their name from a time when people believed that these snakes would drink milk straight from a cow. However, people today know that this is not true. A milk snake does not drink milk, and it would be more likely to slither away from a large cow.

Milk Snakes

Milk snakes are smaller than both corn and king snakes. By the time milk snakes reach adulthood, they usually are less than 3 feet long (.91 m).

Milk snakes have grey or tan bodies with blotches of orange and yellow on their backs. Many milk snakes have rings of color around their bodies. Smooth scales cover the milk snake's skin making it look shiny.

Milk snakes may eat other snakes, so they should be kept in separate terrariums. As with other snakes, milk snakes should be fed small mice. A healthy pet milk snake may live for 15 to 20 years.

Ball Pythons

Pythons are another type of snake that can be kept as pets. Ball pythons are the most common pet pythons. They grow to be about 5 feet (1.52 m) in length. These grayish brown and black snakes can be kept in tanks that are at least 30 to 40 gallons. Their homes should be about 83 degrees F (28.33 degrees C) during the day and about 76 degrees F (24.44 degrees C) at night. During the day, these snakes do need a

Ball pythons get their name from the way they curl up into a tight ball.

special **basking** spot in their terrariums where the temperature is about 90 degrees F (32.22 degrees C). Ball pythons eat small mice and small rats, and are most active at night.

There are other types of pythons that can be kept as pets, but they are larger in size and require more specialized care. These pythons are not recommended for first-time snake owners.

Certain types of pythons, such as reticulated and Burmese pythons, are better for an experienced snake keeper. Besides the fact that these snakes can grow to be very large, they can sometimes be picky eaters and may be hard to handle.

Boa Constrictors

There are many different types of boa constrictors that can be kept as pets. Many breeders and experts do not recommend a boa as a first snake for an inexperienced snake keeper. But red-tailed boas and rainbow boas are often kept as pets. These boas, however, can grow to be 8 to 10 feet (2.44 to 3.05 m) long. Adolescent and adult boas can weigh as much as 50 pounds (22.7 kilograms).

Snakes of this size need a very large terrarium. When you buy a baby

Rainbow boas have shiny scales and coloring that sometimes make them look like their skin reflects a rainbow of different colors.

boa, you should be ready to care for it for the rest of its life. This means making sure you always have space for its cage or terrarium, and accepting that this kind of snake gets very big. It takes two or more people to safely handle a large boa. Boa constrictors use their strong bodies to constrict, or squeeze, the food they are going to eat. So it is possible for a large boa to hurt—and even kill—a human or a household pet, like a dog or cat, if it gets wrapped around and starts to squeeze. Boas can make good pets, but you have to be well informed and ready to handle their needs.

Instead of attacking or biting, most wild garter snakes prefer to slither away from a human. This does not mean that garter snakes from the wild make good pets.

Garter Snakes

Garter snakes are one of the most common snakes found all over the world. The snake you see in your backyard would most likely be a garter snake. These snakes do not get very big, but they can grow to be 3 feet (.91 m) or longer. Most garter snakes have colored stripes that run down their backs or sides. In the wild, garter snakes that live around the water eat small frogs and fish. Those that live in people's gardens eat earthworms. A pet garter snake would eat very small mice, fish, worms, or some types of insects.

Garter snakes are active during the day, so you could spend a lot of time watching them go about their activities. With patience and care, most garter snakes can be handled. But unlike corn, milk, or king snakes, garter snakes will not move slowly around your hand or through your fingers. These snakes move quickly and straighten their body a lot as they move around. As a result, they can sometimes be hard to handle.

If you are unsure of what kind of snake to buy, take your time and do more research. Visit reptile shows or contact reptile societies. Buying any kind of pet should not be a quick decision. Picking the right kind of pet snake will lead to many happy years with your slithering friend.

Always try to learn as much as you can before settling on a pet snake. Some nature centers and reptile societies offer opportunities for you to learn about and handle different types of snakes.

4

Caring for Your Snake

Once you have decided to get a snake, know which kind of snake you want and where you will get it, you should start preparing its home. It is important to have all the supplies ready and set up before you bring your snake home.

Creating an Enclosed Habitat

Unlike a dog or cat, pet snakes should never be allowed to roam freely throughout your home. Snakes like to squeeze into small spaces, so they can get stuck somewhere dangerous or somewhere where you cannot reach it, like between the walls of your home. Small snakes can be stepped on, hurt, or bitten by other household pets. Larger snakes may do the opposite and use your smaller pets as food. This is why snakes should be kept in an enclosure when they are not being handled or closely watched.

Handling your pet snake will help to make it tame. But when you are not holding it, your pet should be safely enclosed in its terrarium or cage.

The size of the enclosure, terrarium, case, or cage that you will need depends on the size of the snake that you choose. All snakes start out small, but some grow bigger and longer than others. When the snakes are very small you can use a small tank or terrarium. But as they get larger you must provide them with a larger enclosure. Pet stores and reptile shows sell a variety of snake enclosures. Some people even make their own enclosures for their snakes. Regardless of what you decide to do, you must make sure that the terrarium is large enough, allows enough air to circulate, and can be closed so that the snake cannot escape. Many first-time snake keepers find that fish tanks, or aquariums, are the best homes for their new snakes. Just make sure that it is large enough and has a locking cover that will keep the snake from getting out.

After you have the case, you will need to fill it with items that the snake can use. These include rocks, branches (if your snake naturally likes to climb trees and wrap around branches), and some kind of cave or enclosed space where it can hide and feel safe. You should get these supplies from a pet store, a reptile show, or a breeder. Do not get branches or rocks from outdoors. The rocks and branches may have chemicals from the lawn—such as pesticides or fertilizers—or they may have insects or other little organisms that can hurt your snake. All the supplies you put into the case should be easy to clean.

The bottom of your snake cage or tank should have some sort of **substrate**, or floor covering. This gives the snake something to move around on or burrow in. It also absorbs waste that comes from your snake's body. Experts recommend newspaper, pine bark chips, or aspen wood shavings as the

Pine bark chips are used as a substrate in this king snake's cage.

substrate for most snake enclosures. All of these can be bought at pet stores. These types of substrates are good because they can be easily cleaned and replaced as needed.

One of the best suggestions for a substrate is fake grass or Astroturf. Experienced snake keepers suggest keeping at least two pieces of Astroturf that fit on the floor of the enclosure. One piece stays inside the cage until it is time to be cleaned. You can then replace it with the second, clean piece while you clean the first piece. Astroturf is a good choice because it is easy to wash, not too expensive, and the snake cannot accidentally eat it with its food.

Heat, Light, and Humidity

Because snakes are cold-blooded animals, they rely on their environment to control their body temperatures. As the snake's caretaker, you need to provide your pet with the right amount of heat. Special heating elements for snakes can be used to heat your snake's home. These heating elements plug into an electrical outlet for energy. Reptile heating elements can be bought from a pet store or reptile show.

Never put your snake's home in the sunlight or in front of a fireplace, heating vent, or space heater. Even though those are sources of heat, they can make your snake too hot and hurt it. Special snake heaters allow you to control your snake's environment so that it can be

This python coils around the branches in its cage so that it can absorb the heat and light it needs to survive.

comfortable. Dark hiding places within the enclosure will allow your snake to hide when it wants privacy and to cool down when it is feeling hot. Different types of snakes need different temperatures during the day and night. Check with a breeder or a veterinarian to find out what temperature is good for your snake.

Snakes also need light. This light provides some warmth, but it also will help them with their daily schedules. Snakes that are active during the day need the light to go about their daily activities. Snakes that are active at night know to be active when there is no daylight. This does not mean that

Snakes do not have very good eyesight. To sense things in their environments, snakes use their tongues. The tongue flicks out and tests the air, telling the snake if there are certain smells or tastes it should be aware of. Snakes can also sense heat around them. That is one way they hunt—by judging where their prey is based on the smaller animal's body heat.

This python uses its forked tongue to sense the particles in the air around it.

nocturnal snakes (which are active at night) should be in the dark at night. There are special bulbs that can be used so that you can still see your snake, without exposing it to light that is like daylight.

Snakes also need a certain amount of **humidity**, or moisture in the air, in their enclosures. This can usually be controlled by adjusting the temperature and providing a dish of water. With the right amount of heat, the water in the dish will evaporate and put moisture into the air. Too much moisture can hurt the snake, so be sure to check with a breeder or veterinarian for humidity requirements for your breed of snake.

Food

The amount and the number of times you feed your snake depend on the age and size of your pet. Talk to a breeder or a veterinarian to find out what a proper diet for your new pet should be. Most pet snakes eat small animals, usually mice or small rats. Pet snakes should never be fed live animals. A live mouse or rat can bite and hurt your pet snake. Instead, snake keepers feed their snakes pre-killed frozen mice or rats. There are several benefits to feeding your snake this kind of food. The animal is already dead, so you will not have to kill it and it cannot hurt your snake. Buying frozen mice or rats means that you can keep more of your snake's food in your home for longer periods of time. You do not need to go and find fresh food every time your snake needs to be fed. Pet stores, breeders, and reptile shows sell frozen mice and rats of different sizes.

This corn snake will swallow its meal—a mouse—whole. Though snakes have fangs, they do not use them for chewing.

Snakes do not chew their food. They swallow it whole. So a snake should never be fed food that is wider than the widest part of the snake's body. Small snakes and young snakes should be fed baby mice, which are often called pinkies. Larger mice or rats can be fed to larger snakes. Snakes do not need to eat every day. Most snakes take a few days or more to **digest** their food. Do not handle your snake a lot if it has just eaten. It can be unhappy and may bite, but it may also throw up its food or become sick.

Snakes have jaws that are hooked together by special muscles that stretch. When it eats, a snake can adjust its jaws so that it can open its mouth very wide. This is how it can swallow food that looks much bigger than the snake's head.

Water

Like all animals, snakes need water to survive. A shallow dish of water is ideal for most snakes. They will stick their tongues in and drink when they are thirsty. Some snakes, however, like to soak in water to keep their skin healthy and their bodies cool. These snakes need shallow bowls or tubs that are partially filled with water. The water should be changed regularly, especially if there is substrate, food, or poop in it.

Cleaning Up

Snakes do not eat very much and they do not eat very often, but they still push waste from their body. And this waste needs to be cleaned. Your snake will stay healthier and its enclosure will smell better if you remove whatever your snake has not eaten about one hour after you feed it. Any waste material it pushes out needs to be removed every day. If you have a substrate like aspen shavings, pine chips, or newspaper, you can just scoop up the parts that are wet and dirty. For Astroturf, you can just wipe up the dirty spots.

KEEPING IT CLEAN

Never wash your snake enclosure or supplies in a kitchen or bathroom sink. The germs and dirt from the snake's supplies can make humans sick. The best place to wash the snake supplies is in a tub or outside with a hose. If you use the tub, be sure to scrub it with a disinfectant soap afterward.

Handwashing is also very important. Always wash your hands after you handle your snake or any of its supplies. It is also important to wash your hands before holding your snake. Some types of human germs can also make snakes sick. Practicing good cleanliness habits will help to keep you and your snake healthy.

At least once a month you should clean your snake's entire enclosure. (You should do this more often if your snake tends to make a mess throughout the enclosure.) First, put your snake somewhere safe where it cannot get hurt or escape. Then take out all pieces inside the enclosure and wash them with very hot water. While those pieces are drying, wash out the inside of the tank or cage to make sure that all dirt and waste is gone. Dry the enclosure and fill it with the new substrate or with a clean piece of Astroturf. Once everything is back to normal, put your snake back inside and give it a little while to get used to its cleaner surroundings.

Snake Health

If you are not sure if your snake is sick or if you need advice on how to care for your snake, a veterinarian, or vet for short, can be your best resource.

A vet can take care of your snake when it gets sick.

Before bringing home your snake, find the contact information for a vet in your area. You must be sure that the vet treats snakes, because not all vets do. You can find names of vets that treat snakes on the Internet, in snake magazines, or through reptile societies and breeders.

Shedding

As snakes grow, they need to grow new skin. As new skin comes in, old skin is **shed,** or slowly comes off. For young snakes who are growing fast,

This corn snake is slowly shedding its skin. Snakes can be grumpy or hard to hold before and while they are shedding, so handle them with care.

Having a slithering, scaly, reptilian pet can be a lot of fun.

shedding their skins happens a few times each year. First, the scales over the snake's eyes grow dull, or less shiny. Then all the scales on the snake's body do the same thing. The old skin starts to peel off, usually in big pieces. Sometimes a snake will shed its entire skin in one whole piece! When they are shedding, snakes may rub against rocks or branches inside their enclosures. When it is done shedding, the snake looks like it did before, and thin, white- or yellow-colored skin will be left in the enclosure. Snakes usually do not need help while they are shedding so do not try to pull off the old skin. Not only can you hurt the snake, but you may get bitten. If you think your snake is having problems shedding, contact a vet and ask for advice.

Like any other pet, snakes are fun to watch, to touch, and to feed. And although all pets need care, snakes are very special. They require special habitats and have specific needs when it comes to food. Though they are not furry or fluffy like other pets, snakes can be as much fun to hold and handle. With the right amount of patience, care, and time, keeping a pet snake can be a unique and fun experience.

Glossary

bask—To stay still and absorb light or heat. Snakes need to bask to warm their bodies.

breeder—Someone who raises specific types of animals.

digest—To break down food so it can be used for energy.

habitat—Where an animal lives.

humidity—The amount of moisture in the air.

shedding—To get rid of something. Snakes shed their skin.

species—A specific type of animal. For example, boa constrictors and corn snakes are two different snake species.

substrate—The floor covering for your snake's enclosure.

terrarium—A container used as a habitat for a pet.

venom—A chemical that some types of snakes use to hurt or kill their prey or to protect themselves when they are in danger.

veterinarian—A doctor that treats animals—often called a vet for short.

Find Out More

Books

Craats, Rennay. *Caring for Your Snake*. New York: Weigl Publishers, 2005.

Feldman, Heather. *Milk Snakes*. New York: PowerKids Press, 2004.

Hernandez-Divers, Sonia. *Snakes*. Chicago: Heinemann Library, 2003.

Whiting, Jim. *Care for a Pet Snake*. Hockessi, DE: Mitchell Lane Publishers, 2008.

Web Sites

About Snakes
http://www.aboutsnakes.com
This Web site answers a lot of questions about snakes—especially about pet snakes. There is information on how to choose a snake and how to care for it.

Reptile and Amphibian Information
http://www.wnyherp.org
This Web site of the Western New York Herpetological Society has a lot of information about caring for different types of pet snakes.

Snakes as Pets
http://exoticpets.about.com/cs/snakes/a/snakesaspets.htm
The articles on this Web site were written by a veterinarian and offer good advice and information for people who are either first-time snake keepers or are considering getting a snake as a pet.

Snake Tips
http://www.boatips.com/cornsnakes
This Web site has a lot of information about caring for different types of pet snakes.

Index

Page numbers for illustrations are in **bold.**

About the Author

Joyce Hart has written many books for young readers on a variety of
topics. She lives outside of Seattle and often comes across wild snakes
in her garden.